MERCHANDISING FOR BEGINNERS

By Siddique Ali Noor

Merchandising for Beginners Vol:1

Table of Contents

Disclaimer .... Page 03
Shortcut Terms .... Page 04

Chapter 01 .... Page 05
- Title: Merchandiser

Chapter 02 .... Page 07
- Title: Job Responsibilities

  Headers:
  - Good Relationship
  - Stock Availability
  - FIFO (First In- First out)
  - POG (Plano gram)
  - Price Tag & MDR

Chapter 03 .... Page 11
- Title: Share of Shelf

Chapter 04 .... Page 12
- Title: Tips for Creating Effective Display

Chapter 05 .... Page 15
- Title: Some Retailer Rules of Working

Chapter 06 .... Page 16
- Title: Golden Rules & Skills of Merchandiser

Disclaimer

The information in this book/eBook is meant to be used as a guide only. This item is not a licensed product. I do not claim ownership of any character or image used in this book. Copyright and trademarks used of any character/ image used belong to their respective owners are not being sold.

Myself, (Siddique Ali having a Bachelor Degree in Arts) I'm a student and the information is given in this book is based on my experience in this field.

The main purpose of this book/eBook is to provide information and to share knowledge.

No warranties and guarantees are expressed.

For any inquiry or comments, write me at:

siddique.jamali1@gmail.com

Shortcut Terms

Short Form	Complete Term
MDR	Merchandising Daily Report
FMCG	Fast Moving Consumer Goods
R.T.V	Return to Vendor
MSL	Must Stock List or Monthly Sales Index
OSA	On Shelf Availability
FIFO	First In First Out
G-Area	General area where promoted items are displayed
KVI	Known Value Item
P.O	Purchase Order
EOM	End Of Month
SKU	Stock Keeping Unit (A retailer term used to identify each individual product at a unique model or part number)

Chapter 1: Merchandiser?

Whether you are familiar with the word "Merchandiser" or not, most probably it might be a new word for you if you live in a non-western country or a non-English language region.

So, What or who is this merchandiser being said? I have personally been in this field for more than 10 years now and I did love this job. It is an art. I consider this an origin of the customer service work of the product to increase sell.

(Photo of specific category shelf area inside the retailer)

In an active and small definition "Everything that happens to a product from the moment it is delivered to the store to the moment a shopper picks it up off the shelf, this cycle routine task is the said guy", Merchandiser is responsible for this. In other words, by working closely with supplier and manufacturer, a guy that can be responsible for product appearance and supply in various stores shelves and displays throughout their work plan. Depending on the retailer, that may include performing stock outs, organizing the shelf, setting up displays, and setting up the price and promotional signs.

NOTE: Some stores have their own merchandising departments, but others use third-party companies to handle merchandising certain displays. If you are employed by one of these companies, you will need your own reliable transportation to get you to and from each location. You'll travel from store to store setting up displays, working on reports, and talking with employees.

Illustration of G-area (General Area for Promotion Items)

Chapter 2: Job Responsibilities

Major Job responsibilities are divided into five points in my experience & practice:

1: Good Relationship

First things first; it is an art of collaborating work. A good relationship is a condition with everyone you see every day and shake your hand in your field. In my opinion it is not a skill; but I consider it a huge responsibility because you are in nature of work where you face a change every day with new things collaborating with supplier, store to ensure proper execution of plans, winning an extra space in share of shelf, and additional displays such as floor and gandola try their best for the goods should be displayed properly well as to boost the sales.

NOTE: Gandola are secondary space displays that are located in the Start and End of the shelf.

(Illustrations of a Branded (contracted) Gandola.

2: Stock Availability

Visiting outlets ensure product availability, visibility, and receiving deliveries and make sure the products arrive on time and displayed on shelves properly before stock lasts. Start your work in-store plan from promoted item for KVI items; work closely with the display staff in order to decide how goods should be displayed so as to boost the sales to a maximum number.

3: FIFO (First In First Out)

Displaying products with a FIFO system and removing any expired or damaged products, and meeting with store managers for re-ordering products. Products must be taken off the shelf before 30 days of the expiration date.

NOTE: The first-in, first-out (**FIFO**) method of inventory valuation is a cost flow assumption that the first goods purchased are also the first goods sold. In a retail grocery store, this system is very much important due to the expiration date of the product on most items

(Branded/Contracted Stand Display)

4: POG (Plano gram)

Maintain store shelves by applying Plano gram given by the company.

NOTE: A Plano gram is a visual merchandising tool. A supplier pays rent for the space that the products occupy and customers enter and navigate through this floor space before ideally making a purchase. Plano grams are detailed drawings of your share of shelf layout with special attention on product placement. Plano grams helps to plan the use of item space and gather data to help them make smarter visual merchandising choices that drive in-store sales.

(Illustration of Plano gram implemented)

5: Price Tag and MBR

Price tag information must be displayed directly on the product or stickered on shelf bay. You should make sure that all the merchandise is priced; if a customer doesn't see pricing on a product, he will feel uneasy and there is a chance that the customer will leave empty handed without buying your products.

Make and submit your daily MBR (Merchandising Daily Report)

Chapter 3: Share of Shelf

Some call it "Share of Shelf" or "Share of Space". It is an agreement that take place between the retailer and supplier for the rent of space in category shelf in percentage. The supplier pays for it annually or in any term they agreed on.

Below is an example of how can a merchandiser measure or calculate the share of shelf

Percentage:

Share of shelf contract= 10%

Total Shelf Category Shelf by meter = 12meter

10x12=120/100 = 1.2meter block

NOTE: Top to bottom display called block.

Chapter 4: Tips for Creating Effective Display

Following tips should be implemented for creating effective display.

Tip No.1

1. Always display merchandise vertically rather than horizontally.

Tip No.2

2. Eye-Level: This is the most popular concept when it comes to display your product; Eye-level is the best-selling height on every display - as it is the easiest height for shoppers to browse the products.

See illustrations of eye level shelves in the image below.

Tip No.3

3. Apply Color Coordinating formula.

Tip No.4

4. Fill your shelves as much products as possible.

(The picture mentioned above is a bad example of merchandising. Always fill your shelves and in any case if a specific product is not available, fill the other same category SKUs until it re-stocks)

Tip No.5

5. Make sure all the products are priced.

(Floor display with a promo price sign)

Chapter 5: Some Retailer Rules of Working

Becoming a company/supplier merchandiser visiting retailer outlets means you agree to their terms and rules of working. For example a merchandiser must be dressed up with certain given uniform; wearing shoes properly; use the backdoor to enter/exit for personal activities; put your phone and ID to the reception. Moreover, breakfasting, smoking or eating is not allowed in the working area.

Here are some pictures given below that illustrates "Not to-do" activities inside the retailer:

CAUTION: Do not use a jack as a scooter   Do not block a way, keep things aside

CAUTION Arrange your product nicely in the backdoor shelves

Chapter 6: Golden Riles & Skills of Merchandiser

- Choosing a location or space on shelf where your product can be perfectly visible and that make your shelves always fully displayed.
- Have sufficient knowledge about your product as well your competitors.
- Punctuality of time.
- Cleanness is the key.
- Always learn
- Be team-work player.

Final words ;

A big " THANK YOU " for observing and reading this book.

I appreciate if you recommend this book for whoever need this small tiny basics course on merchandising in retail stores.

This book will bring worth of a lot of value in your life/career development because ;

Inside is my ten years experience of this field in a small and short book I have personally authored ;

So much knowledgable ; you could talk confidently and pass the interview and get a job.

Revision Exercise ! (Bonus pages)

After reading the entire chapters of the book, I recommend for my readers to take the recap exercise on next pages with pen/pencil.

Fill in the blanks with correct answers.

OSA is stand for. _____

Full form of FIFO. _____

Full form of FMCG _____

R.T.V means ? _____

MDR stand for. _____

Give little short answers for the following questions.

Q1: Define Planogram ?
Ans:

Q2: What is G-area ?
Ans:

Q3: What is SKU stand for ?
Ans:

Q4: Why it is necessary to implement the system of " FIFO before filling products ?
Ans:

NOTES: